What Happens In Your Home?

I avoid that place
I am not like them
Said Izah to the
school counselor.
She looked
nervous being
pulled into the
counselor office
that day.

"The counselor asked another question "

IZAH IS THERE ANYTHING AT ALL ANTHING STRANGE THAT GOES ON AT HOME?

Izah froze she didn't know what to say she was so afraid to speak. The fear was so overwhelming

THE COUNSELOR LOOKED AT IZAH AND KNEW SOMETHING WAS WRONG AT HOME...

Izah went
back to
class not
sure what
to think...

WILL I REALLY GET IN
TROUBLE IF I TELL A
GROWN UP ABOUT
HOW ME AND MY
SIBLINGS PLAY EACH
OTHER IZAH
WONDERED??

WILL I REALLY GET IN TROUBLE FOR THE WAY MY UNCLE HAS FUN WITH ME WHAT ABOUT THOSE GROWN MEN THAT HAVE FUN WITH ME???

out of

focus

Alone

Afraid

SCARY

story

FEAR

FLOORING

IN

IZASH BEGAN TO FEEL ISOLATED AT HOME, UNSURE OF WHO WOULD SAFEGUARD HER IF SHE CONFIDED IN THE ADULTS AT SCHOOL ABOUT WHAT WAS GOING ON. SHE QUESTIONED WHETHER HER MOTHER WOULD MISTREAT HER IF SHE EVER DISCLOSED WHAT WAS HAPPENING AT HOME. IS IT NORMAL FOR HER UNCLE AND OTHER MEN TO INTERACT WITH HER IN THAT MANNER? WILL SHE FACE CONSEQUENCES FOR SPEAKING OUT? AS IZAH PONDERED THESE QUESTIONS SILENTLY TO HERSELF.

Izah was experincing tons of sexual abuse at home and around to community by the age of 11 years old. To many times kids don't speak because of fear of telling others ...

I can't tell the
truth mommy
will hurt me if
I tell anyone
what happens
in this house.

I don't
think this
is okay
anymore.

If I tell I
am good
as dead.

Go play without me it will be okay.

KNOWING WHAT WAS ABOUT TO HAPPEN I TOLD THEM TO GO PLAY TO KEEP THE PEACE.

Fear over took my body as clothes came off

AND YOUR HOW OLD THE COUNSELOR ASKED IZAH? IZAH ANSWERED 13 YEARS OLD.

Izah this is not okay.

COUNSELOR OKAY JUST DO WHAT YOU NEED TO DO TO SURVIVE.

I can't tell anyone including the school counselor.

WHY NOT BECAUSE THERE WILL BE BLOOD SHED EVERYWHERE.

Counselor told "tell me more about everything that goes on your home.

well my siblings
and I have
touched each
other in sinful
ways

Tell me more about your home life. The counselor stated.

Izah
agreed to
keep
sharing

My Clothes Come Off

THIS HAPPENS WHEN MY UNCLE AND THOSE GROWN MEN GET ME TO DRINK GROWN UP DRINKS

Play time

Can We Stop Now

SURE WOULD YOU LIKE TO SHARE MORE ON A LATER DATE?

Sounds Great then we can talk about the gang activity I will be forced into well I am already involved just not that deep yet.

holy spirit the counselor stated.

Continued

...

Izah is
struggling
with this
reality.

Who do I tell? I might be in trouble.

THIS MAN JUST TRIED TO GIVE ME COCAINE.

You are only allowed to claim our gang my siblings and uncle said

WHEN DID THEY SAY THIS ASKED THE COUNSELOR?

I was around 10 years old. As I got older my friends became more like them apart of the same gang.

I don't want them touching me anymore this isn't right WHAT HAPPENED IZAH?

He made
me take
my
clothes
off.
who did?

My step
brother

DID YOU TELL
ANYONE?

I screamed that's all I could do. No one heard me.

I JUST STOPPED CARING AND STARTED TO LET MY UNCLE SIBLINGS AND MY OTHER FAMILY TOUCH ME TO STAY SAFE.

I AM SO SORRY SWEETIE. I AM HERE TO HELP YOU OK.

Holy spirit I don't think I could do this without you

I KNOW THIS A HARD REALITY TO ACCEPT YOU WILL MAKE IT THROUGH.

Will you
always be
there for
me?

THE HOLY
SPIRIT ANSWER
YES I WILL

How do I
deal with
this?
JUST LISTEN TO
YOUR INNER
VOICE.

What is
that?

IT'S ME THE
HOLY SPIRIT
YOUR GREAT
COUNSELOR

"I Was Sol
I Was Use
Now I am
TRASHE

Children
are a
Gift
Get louder!!

NO MEANS NO

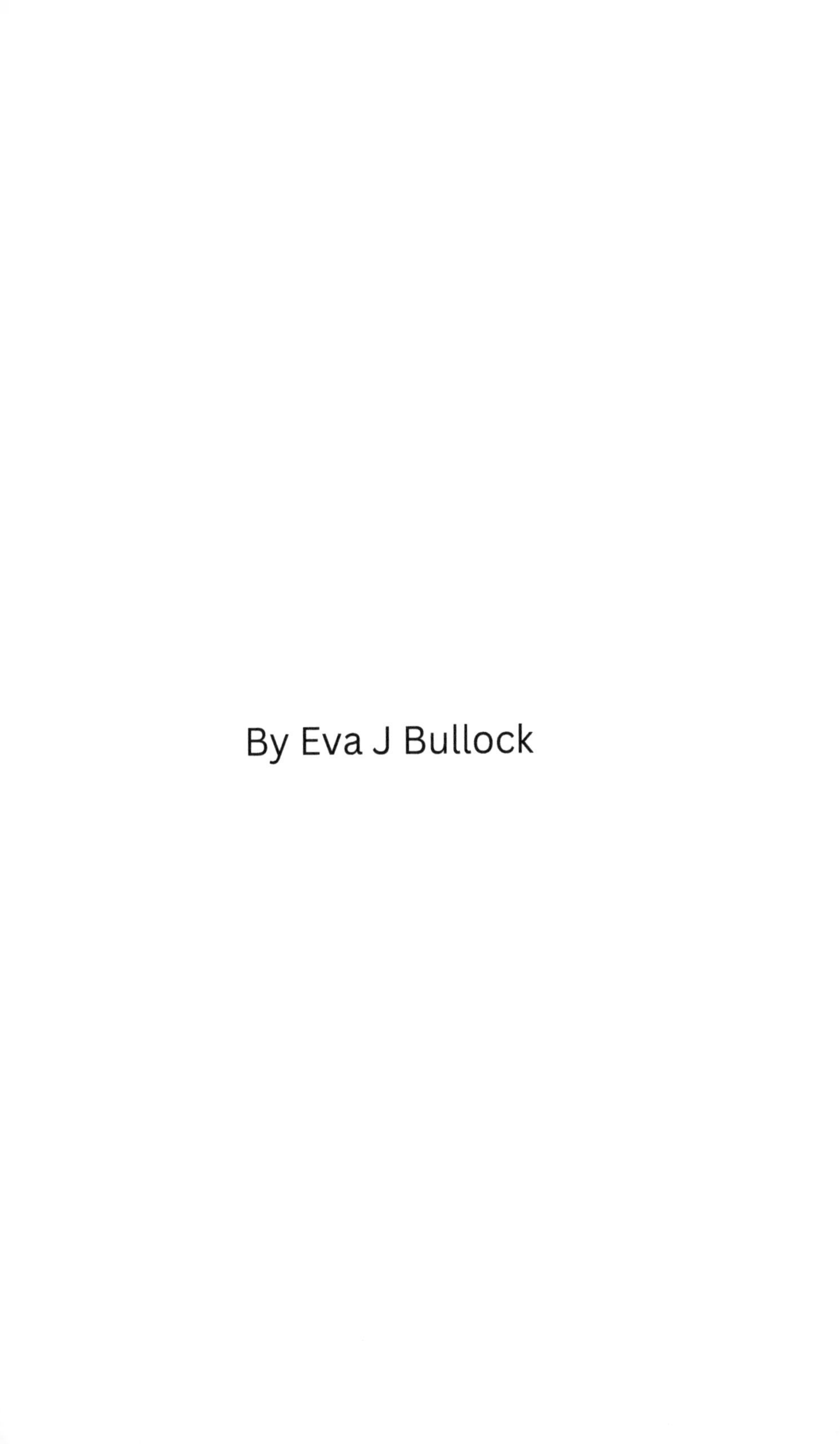

By Eva J Bullock

www.ingramcontent.com/pod-product-compliance
Lightning Source LLC
Chambersburg PA
CBHW041807260726
48664CB00035B/1448